# This Heart is a Haunted House

## casey cowan

to the hopeless romantics. to the believers.
to the overly sensitive. to the forsaken muses.
to everyone that's ever been told they feel too much.

foreword by Kelly Falkner

In *This Heart is a Haunted House*, Casey Cowan proves yet
again she is a fearless navigator of the human experience,
wielding words with a rare depth and clarity that resonate
long after the last page is turned. Each poem is a
testament to her remarkable bravery and brilliant insight.
Her writing is vulnerable and raw with an honesty that
feels both intimate and universal. Casey's grasp of human
emotion offers us a mirror into our own hearts. This
collection is an achingly beautiful offering from a poet
who has indeed found her voice.

content warning:

gentle reminder that this book contains references
to sensitive material relating to:

eating disorders
death
suicidal ideation
grief
sexual assault
& more

# we have to start somewhere

I don't want to say that I'm better
because better feels like forgetting
better seems as though the world kept spinning
when mine stopped on a dime

instead I will say

I have started singing again
only in the car, only
when no one can hear it
my voice may shake but
I have started singing again

instead I will say

I am a little less angry and
a little more hopeful
I feel the sun on my face
my hands are still freezing but
I'm a little less angry

instead I will say

I am writing again
mostly about life
and all it has taken from me
I can't write about you yet but
I am writing again

## the words

I waited for the words to come
for weeks and months and years
I was patient, even when their absence left me hungry
starving for confession
I did not grow weary

# lonely

there are days the loneliness comes
like gentle breezes
like ocean waves
and there are days it comes
like a punch to the stomach
like a knife to the throat

I'm not a violent person but
I'd bloody my knuckles for you
fight off all the hands that still reach for you
because they never held you close enough
when they had the chance
stick needles in the eyes of those
who stare after you
because they didn't see what they had in front of them
all this time

my dear
ten years is an awfully long time to pine
to yearn
to wait
but I'd wait forever if I had to

I wish that I was extraordinary
that I could give you what you so desperately want
but I'm not
and I can't
and I will spend the rest of my life
coming to terms with that

# here's the truth

you are the muse I keep coming back to
the hand that stays outreached for mine
the bridge that no matter how many times it burns
blazes
builds
back to life

you are the ghost I can't outrun
believe me, I've tried
through motorways
and new lips
I accepted long ago
that every time I see you
could be the very last time

you are broken bones
and breaking hearts
shattering glass
and that look on your face
keeps my head spinning
you know the one
when you purse your lips while you play guitar

but I am not the girl you end up with
I am not the goddess worthy of all your pain
I am not the light at the end of the tunnel
or in this case
at the end of your American Spirit cigarette

and that is why I must
let
you
go

# what rhymes with jealousy?

I am jealous of the cigarette between your lips
the tattoo on your ribs
and the people you actually miss

# day drinking

I've started day drinking
wine, rum, tequila, anything
that eases the sting of abandonment
you'd think by now I would be used to this
we happened a lifetime ago

the jukebox plays Led Zeppelin
and I picture you
racing down backroads
windows down, singing wildly
hitting all the wrong notes
but you smile and suddenly
I can't hear anything at all
everything and everyone that's not us dissolves

somewhere a glass breaks
and I am jolted back to reality
I know there's a metaphor there somewhere
but I just keep sipping my drink

they say you're doing better
you're in love…again
the masochist in me wonders
if she knows anything about me at all
but then, I remember that
I'm just a ghost of a girl you used to know
an animal who sank its teeth in and refused to let go

sure, the scar's still there but now
it's just a story of how you survived me
a testament of your strength

*can I get another drink?*

# the boy i loved at seventeen

I am always hyper aware that it's your birthday
year after year my most dreaded holiday creeps up on me
mom called earlier and asked about my plans
do you remember when you called her mother too?
I had to fight the bubbling in my throat
that tries to scream your name
but instead I just say,
*"oh just groceries and errands! there's so much to do!"*
I wish I could be as oblivious as her
she has already forgotten you
lucky

I heard you got a whole new life by the end of last summer
I don't know why I was surprised
you've always been good at starting over
tell me, do you hold a funeral for your former persona?
I am haunted by the ease in which you forget me

you said I was the only consistency that you'd ever had
and my stupid ass took it as a compliment
Ashley once said that warning signs feel like butterflies
and I think that she was right

your birthday is over, and I can finally catch my breath
but time keeps moving faster every year that we grow older
do you see my ghost when you look over your shoulder?
am I haunting you the way you're haunting me?

someday, if this reaches you somehow
there's one thing I want you to remember
you are the worst person I have ever met
and I wish it was me who could forget

# are you there?

maybe it's wishful thinking/maybe it's that I haven't slept in three days/but I keep waiting for you to come back/pacing back and forth/now it's 11 pm on a Sunday and I'm wondering where you are/we haven't spoken since February twenty twenty one /I haven't seen your face except in memories I can't outrun/it's the way you hide from my heart like it's a loaded gun/I'm coming undone/I hear you in the static/in the white noise/in the traffic/and the songs have only ever been about you/I'm sure I seem delusional/I think I've been possessed/a victim of a spell/but god I must confess/despite what you believe there's no halo around my head/I'm so far off the ground/you seem so far away/and I would fall from grace/just to put a smile on your face/always seemed so sad/sad eyes like mine/I think the fates have got it wrong I swear the stars aligned/but it's fine/I rehearse what I'd say to you every night at four am/the moon wakes me up/and the wolves sing our hymns/I've said goodbye in dreams and wished you well I swear/sometimes I have to ask myself if you were ever really there

how perfectly romantic would that be?
we both wear our demons like charms on a bracelet
like scars on our wrists

# a new circle of hell

I do not talk about you often

no one in my life now knows anything about you
your name but a curse on my lips
a secret that belongs to me
I do my best not to even think about you

but memory is a blade
and I keep slicing myself open
violent lacerations
merely a flesh wound
it's all the same

I bottle up all the blood as an offering
gift you my cold, wretched heart
make a solemn vow
I was yours then and now

I am afraid I will always feel your absence
we're a game of cat and mouse
and our home is just a house
I boarded up the windows
for sale sign on the lawn
because it's not just me you haunt

I don't know if I can love someone like I loved you
like I love you still
and that in itself is a new circle of hell

# the poet drops the bullshit
# and cuts the tether loose

I used to tell you stories to help you fall asleep, remember?
always with the light on, usually in 7th period geometry
I think we were made of matches from the start
maybe you just set fires to cover your tracks

forced to fight for your affection
bruised and broken knuckles
screaming "put 'em up, kid"
I worked so hard to earn it
to deserve it
but acing all your tests never made a difference

it's been a few years
and you've found a new girl
and while you still circle the drain
in my brain
I mostly think of your discarded lovers
the forsaken muses

here's to the women you vilify
the jealous and the crazy
the whores and the traitors
the obsessed psycho bitches you just happened to survive

# let's call her starving

blue eyes, ebony mess of hair
skin and bones, I call her
she gets a little irrational
when I start putting all her
dirty little secrets
down on paper
personally
I think she likes the attention

I never need the apps
she counts every calorie for me
"did you really need that or are you just fat?"
sometimes I want to tell her to get lost
but loneliness is a bitch
and it's nice to have one reliable friend

# like a venom

sometimes it feels
like I'm going to get
lost in this illness
as if who I am will be
consumed
by counting calories
and hitting my step count
I wish I could just eat
that my mind wouldn't race
obsess over every minuscule detail

but it's my mind that's the monster
she's deadly like a weapon
like a venom
I'm afraid of her
I think she likes it that way

I.

What is reality but something I'm unable to grasp?
something sticky somehow sliding between my fingers
I swear I'm staring at the chalkboard but everything is

~~blurry~~
~~muddy~~
~~foggy~~

all the damn time
    *can you tell me the time?*

II.

what do you do,
when you look at a photo but the photo's not you?
not who you are, not who you see
*the person standing there looks nothing like me!*
they never tell you
that mirrors can lie
and selfies? ugh
snapchat's the worst

III.

I say,

*I'm stuck in a space between*
    *shame and salvation*

they say,

  *you're not trying hard enough*

please tell me how hard I have to try
before I can look myself in the eye
no quivering lip, no sweaty palms
safe


IV.

what is reality but a locked front door?
the kitchen light is on, the car is in the drive
but I'm always looking in from the outside

*what is reality what is time what is on the other side*

what is me
          without you?

# hometowns

train horns and trailer parks
the only thing you see more than churches
broken windows and water leaks
carnival kids and bottles of coke

this town attracts strays like flies to death
they can smell all the blood

I can still smell all the blood

# safe

for months now

I have been one suitcase and phone call away from leaving

only the essentials, let everything else

disintegrate with the house

with no sense of self nor direction I say

anywhere but here

because the walls of our home have started

closing in

on me

your bedroom light flickers

I smell gas in the kitchen

it's not safe here


not anymore

# the poet apologizes to her body

for overfilled stomach aches
for binging and purging
for binging and not purging
for the days of only eating seven saltine crackers
for the days of eating everything in sight
for allowing the same sick cycle of assured destruction
down the rabbit hole I never quite made my way out of

for the first time my mother noticed the stretch marks
growing on my inner thighs
for the way they stretched across my body
tiny, purple lightning bolts cracking over
the body that used to belong to me
for the way the word diet tastes in my mouth
for the way I can't remember the sound of my nana's voice
but I can remember every meal I've ever had

for the lump in my throat when my best friend told me
she would hate me if I ever 'got skinnier than her'
for the lump in my throat that's still there when she's not
for all the times my demons come out to play
for every good thing I've done wrong
for every bad thing I've done right

# violent acts

it feels like the world should stop moving
maybe this is hell and—
                            wait


let me start from the beginning


the wake up call from hell
your lungs fell, only time will tell
mom and dad were sick too, could hardly move
it's up to me to get to you
and I stood there watching you
hooked up to a breathing tube in a makeshift room
but I can't go in and I have to leave soon
even still, I fight with the nurse and pray the medicine works
I still hope for the best when things turn for the worst
I waved at you once through a tiny windowpane
but you couldn't wave back
because your hands were in restraints
I called your hospital room just to talk to you
even though I knew you couldn't talk back
I prayed every single night that you make it through


I don't pray anymore


I thought the first call was bad, no it wasn't even close
now the world is on fire, all up in smoke
the doctor said this was the most violent thing he had ever seen
if only he knew the violent things I'd do
to bring you back to me

# prayer

they say I should pray more
that I should give it to God
well this is my screaming toward the heavens
knees bent, scraped and bloody
for all things holy
what have I missed?
I watched him die
S
  L
   O
    W
    L
     Y

in a hospital bed
I saw him reach for me
and I could not save him

*why couldn't I save him?*

# grief is an old friend who has come to bury the hatchet

I meet my grief for coffee on the corner of Magnolia and Third
their choice, not mine
I don't drink caffeine these days
but Grief insists this is the place to be
at first we sit quietly
I fidget, I never know quite what to do with my hands
and it's been a long time
the only thing I'm better at than running
is pretending it never happened
but Grief smiles and waits

"I've been really angry."
I try to stay calm but of course I'm crying now
Grief nods, and hands me a tissue
"I begged them not to take him. To take me instead."

I try to slow my breathing but I feel as
though I'm being held underwater

"I'm really sad. Two years have passed and I don't know how.
I swear everything stopped at 1:31"

Grief places their hands on mine
and the heat from the summer sun
doesn't burn quite like it did

I don't reduce his death to a lesson I had to learn
but I learned it nonetheless
I can't tell you for certain
why good people die young
or where they go when it's said and done

but

to know him
to live on this floating rock at the same time as him
was a gift
and I think of him often
not only when I'm sad
I think the greatest gift I can give back
is to give life complete and utter
hell

# google search history
# when i can't sleep

Signs of clinical depression/Am I manic?/How to stop missing
someone/How to be happy/the definition of insane/how to
move across the country with no job or money or life skills/I
miss you/am I manic or am I just happy???/symptoms of
ptsd/signs of emotional eating/am I manic or am I just
happy????/how to stop feeling numb/work from home jobs/ i
hate my job/is anyone there?

## there are these things i do
## when i find myself missing you

I put on your deodorant
buy peaches just to watch them rot
spend my days in your favorite t-shirt
I watch the big bang theory

      sometimes I can still hear you laugh

I dig through photos of you
starry eyed at sixteen

      is there a possibility I'm anything like you?

mostly I just pretend
I fully believe
that I'll see you again

# i guess i lied

when I said
that you were the worst person that I'd ever met
with all the monsters and manipulators
the wolves disguised as sheep

most days it's so hard to believe
that we're both no longer seventeen
and I know what they say
about love at that age
our story's been over
but I'm still on that fucking page

do you remember the letter you wrote me on August 27th?
I reread our old conversations
like scripture by a praying man
I pick petals off all the flowers I bought
"he loves me, he loves me not"

I guess I lied when I said
that I wish you were someone I could forget
and I know it's probably
only because your birthday's next week
but I can't sleep

# sad girl hours

fingers, deep in the mud
hair, dirty and matted
teeth, crooked and unbrushed
pick yourself up
slowly, at first
daylight is breaking, birds are singing
that goddamn alarm is going off but everything stays dark
dishes, unwashed and piling up
dust, covering my favorite pictures like a heavy coat
laundry, still on the floor covered in blood
pick yourself up
faster, now
light creeps underneath the curtains—around the edges
but I can't see in front of me
go to therapy, take your meds,
smoke with your friends, avoid them instead
are you drinking enough water?
are you getting enough sleep?
have you been to the gym?
try and go for a walk
go out with your friends and don't even talk
revel in the silence
and shake in the dark
you seem so sad lately
and life's not that fucking hard!
pick yourself up
slowly, at first
faster, now

# sinking ship

I am surrounded by a sea of people
that love me unconditionally
and yet, I get so afraid
that once they see the dysfunction
the destruction
they will leave and take everything they see

darling, you are always going on about light and grace
but I can't see a thing
it's all dark here
give me balance
give me a ship that for once
does not feel like sinking

# another shitty love poem

this heart is full of cobwebs
it's black and it's been blue
a lot of space has been taken up
but I'd make room for you

# mirror mirror

I've got a laundry list of sins
up to my elbows in regret
such a nasty, impenetrable marsh
everything smells like sulfur, sex, and betrayal

but I'm the queen of crossing boundaries
of fast lies, white lies, elaborate lies
so many goddamn lies
would I even know the truth if it looked me in the eyes?

I am all violence, no victim
I am destructive—long since corrupted
so much chaos trapped in such a small cage

if happiness is a choice
I've been too busy choosing ~~you~~
and I spend so much time pondering
when I'll meet my bitter end
will it be catastrophic, like a bridge collapse?
or will it be quiet and soft, simply drowning in past
mistakes I've made, gray in every shade
intensity on high

there are not enough words
to effectively say I'm sorry

I'm sorry for betraying you
I'm sorry for using you
I'm sorry for lying to you
I'm sorry for leaving you

spilling out of me faster
than the blood that's on my hands
like the blood of all my friends

# what i'm most afraid to say

is that I'm afraid
so afraid of everything now
I am terrified to let myself lean into happiness
only to have the rug pulled out from under me again
happiness
a feeling so far in the distance now
but I remember the taste

if we're gonna do this
then fuck it, let's lay it all out
all of my skeletons, all of my dark
I guess you could say
I'm afraid I'm too hard to love
but why do I need it so badly?
I work so hard to earn it, to prove I deserve it
I'm hungry for your heart

I am afraid I will never trust myself
that it will never be enough
that I will keep fighting the same demons
for years and years to come
I read self help books and starve myself
but the girl staring back at me
still feels like somebody else
I am most afraid of how unafraid I feel
and sure, you could blame it on the mania, my grief,
or a hundred other things

all I know is that flirting with danger
feels like playing with fire
and I am soaked
head to toe in gasoline

I could tell you all day of which I'm afraid
because fear has made a home inside of me
an uninvited guest I've asked to leave
am I really the monster my mind believes me to be?

# hush

the stairs groan like they have something to grieve
despite the careful climb
the lights dim and eventually die
darkness swallowing the room whole

the sheets give a disgruntled sigh
start to sweat at the warmth of the invader
the crashing of the atmosphere of their delicate,
yet scratchy fabric

heavy clothes hit the hardwood like bricks
hard enough to shake the dust
hidden on the headboard
the clock on the nightstand shudders at every

stop!

STOP!

STOP!

STOP!

# this was never my fight until it had to be

"you should have known better."

 "what did you think was going to happen?"

set the scene:

I said hi, 'cause I'm polite
I even said it with a smile
but no, you're right,
I walked up to you
and I said it with a smile
now I'm the one on trial
you lied about your relationship
and even about your name
but if I ever told a soul
I'd be the one they'd blame
I wish that I was brave

how hard must I scrub my skin
to never feel your hands again?
let me boil in a bathtub, burn me at the stake
sometimes I still hear you breathing
I can still see your face
this was never my fight
until it had to be

didn't they teach you that coercion
is not consent and it never will be?
didn't they tell you about women like me?

# this heart is a haunted house

there's a part of me
that's banging on the walls
of the cage that is my body
screaming, clawing
trying not to drown
begging for someone
anyone
to listen

no matter how hard I try
to scrub away the fingerprints
you can still feel the residue
of their blistering hands
you can still see the scars

you could say I was a bird
who knows its wings are broken
but can still be found
barreling off of buildings

I am cotton candy softness
melts in the palm of your hand
sugar sweet, I'll rot your teeth

watch me detonate
I'll burn your cities to the ground

this heart is a haunted house
and these chains have names
guilt and shame
and fear clamped tight around my throat

I still wake to tip toed footsteps
and jump at the slightest sounds
but I am a force of nature
and my power knows no bounds

# the end of the world

we live in a world where my mother asks me
to take my mace when taking a walk to clear my head
where I clutch my keys between my fingers
and check for monsters over my shoulder

we live in a world inside a screen
where nothing is real and nothing is free
but there's not much money can't buy
and we use all our energy just to survive
because who has time to be creative, right?

gone are the days of making mistakes
of fucking up and figuring it out
you're going to be perfect and
you're going to do it with everyone watching you

we put big, bad men in the white house
they live like kings
and lock the minorities out
more innocent people die every day
but when it's people of color, they look the other way
they fund wars and pray to their greed
but no one is safe until we're all free
we've lost count of the children who've died
God, who the fuck funds a genocide?
this world is on fire and they tell me to pray
but is 'thoughts and prayers' all you have to say?
we live in a world I will fight to make better

# a letter from my heart

hi

      me again


I can't count how many times you've had to stitch me up
forgive me, for putting you through hell so many times
walk through the fire with me,

                    won't you?

just once more


you wear your loneliness like a favorite perfume
it clings to you
it lingers and fades
cuts like a blade
memorable


you've been at war for years now
traipsing through the bloody battlegrounds of your mind
the gruesome dogfight with your body

             are you ever coming home?

# a poem in which i find my way back

I wouldn't say that I'm better
but see, I have found my voice
however shaky
still knows the melody
won't you sing with me?

I can feel the words stirring in my fingertips
crashing onto the page
so perfectly
feels like home to me

when you live so long
in the darkest nights
without even the moon to keep you company
it's a dangerous kind of melancholy
sort of like a drug to me

I've been shattering walls
breaking down doors
how else can I let the light out?
bathe me in this incandescent glow
is there somewhere only we can go?

I cannot say that I'm better
with a mind like mine
it changes all the time
have you gotten my letters?

the girl in the mirror sort of resembles me now
staring at a stranger for so long
I'd forgotten my own face
but see,
same sad eyes, same crooked teeth

I may not be where I need to go
but at least I'm on the road

Thank you Kelly Falkner, for lending me your beautiful words, for your lifelong love and support, your encouragement. The world is so much brighter with people like you in it. I'm so grateful to know you. I love you. Thank you xx

Thank you to my incredible friends. The love and support you've shown me is nothing short of magical and I thank my lucky stars for you every day.

Thank you to my family. Thank you, mom, for being my best friend in the entire world. For loving me even when that was hard to do. I love you so much.

And to you, reader. Writing has always been my lifeline. Somewhere along the way I got caught up in whether my writing was 'good enough' to be on these pages. Somehow, I made my way back here and it feels so good to be home. Thank you for being so kind, and so eager to hear what I have to say. It means more to me than I could ever tell you. I hope you'll let me give you a hug in person! I love you, dear reader. always.

Made in the USA
Columbia, SC
07 December 2024

47527333R00036